GOD'S CREATURES
AT THE SEASHORE

GOD'S CREATURES
AT THE SEASHORE
His Great Creation

by
Debra K. Stuckey

Illustrated by
Jules Edler

Publishing House
St. Louis

Copyright © 1986 Concordia Publishing House
3558 S. Jefferson Avenue, St. Louis, MO 63118-3968
Manufactured in the United States of America

Library of Congress Cataloging-in-Publication Data

Stuckey, Debra K., 1959-
  God's creatures at the seashore.

  Summary: Describes useful physical characteristics God gave the animals that live at the seashore.

  1. Marine fauna—Religious aspects—Christianity—Juvenile literature. 2. Creation—Juvenile literature. [1. Marine animals] I. Edler, Jules, ill. II. Title.

BT746.S77   1986   231.7'65   85-17104

ISBN 0-570-04133-3

1   2   3   4   5   6   7   8   9   10   PP   95   94   93   92   91   90   89   88   87   86

**To
Rachel and Joshua**

Oh, what a wonderful world
God has made! Many of His
creatures live at the
sheashore.
They help me see
how great God is.

God taught the seagull to
soar gracefully.
I like to toss him
bread crumbs.
He can catch them
in his beak.

God gave the sea otter
warm, thick fur.
It helps him to float
on the water.
He can even float while
he eats or sleeps.

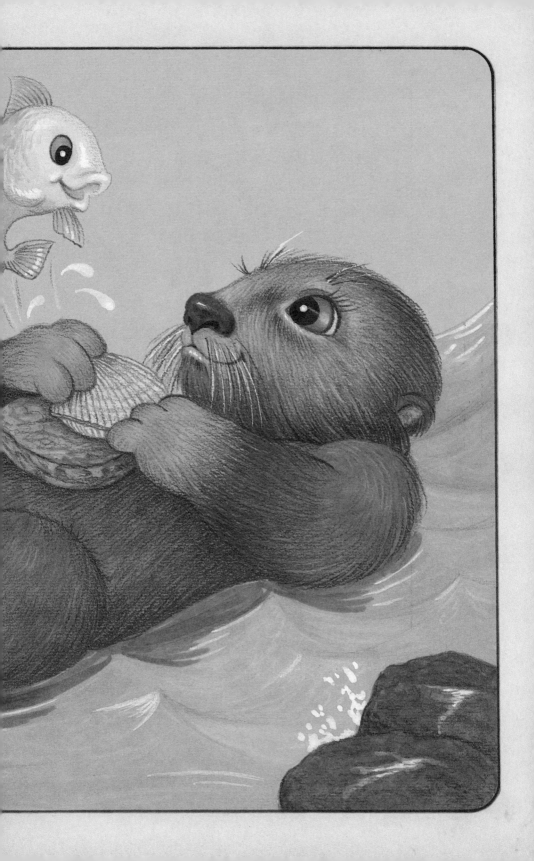

Look at the funny beak
God gave the pelican.
He needs it to catch fish.
He can scoop them right
out of the ocean.

Under the sand, I find a
tiny sand crab.
He is too fast for me to catch.
God taught him to quickly
burrow into the sand.

Slow Mr. Turtle can't run
away fast.
God gave him a hard shell
to hide in.
Are you in there,
Mr. Turtle?

The clam is a muscle inside
two shells.
God made him very strong.
I can't pull him open.
Can you?

The starfish has one, two,
three, four, five arms.
See the tiny suction cups God
put on them?
The starfish uses them to open
the strong, little clam.

See the jellyfish floating on
the waves.
God gave him long tentacles
to catch fish.
Don't touch the tentacles.
They may sting.

Isn't our great God
wonderful?
Everywhere I look, I see
what He has made.
How big and powerful He is!

Thank You, God!
THE END